Staying Healthy:

Let's Exercise!

Alice B. McGinty

The Rosen Publishing Group's
PowerKids Press™
New York

Published in 1997 by The Rosen Publishing Group, Inc.
29 East 21st Street, New York, NY 10010

First Edition

Book Design: Kim Sonsky

Photo Illustrations: Cover and all photo illustrations by Seth Dinnerman.

McGinty, Alice B.
     Staying healthy: Exercise / Alice B. McGinty.
       p.   cm. (The library of healthy living)
     Summary: Defines exercise, describes its benefits, and gives a few examples of how to exercise.
     ISBN 0-8239-5137-5
     1. Exercise—Juvenile literature. 2. Physical fitness for children—Juvenile literature. 3. Exercise for children—Juvenile literature. [1. Exercise. 2. Physical fitness.] I. Title. II. Series.
     QP301.M3753 1996
     613.7'1—dc21
                                                                96-47208
                                                                     CIP
                                                                       AC

Manufactured in the United States of America

Contents

Exercising Your Body

You can do amazing things. You can walk, run, and jump. You can lift, stretch, and climb. You can move!

Your body *needs* to move. Your body needs **exercise** (EX-er-syz) to be healthy and strong.

There are many ways to exercise. Exercise can be pedaling a bike, hopping, dancing, throwing a ball, swimming, jumping rope, and playing soccer.

What kinds of exercise do you like to do?

Your Bones and Joints

Each time you move, many things happen inside your body.

When you kick a ball, your leg bends. But the bones in your body are hard and straight. How does your leg bend?

Your leg is made of several bones, connected at your knee. Your knee is a **joint** (JOYNT). Joints are the places where the bones in your body connect. They are the places where you can bend and move.

Exercise helps make your joints **flexible** (FLEX-ih-bul) and strong so you can move easily.

Your joints, such as knees, elbows, shoulders, and wrists, allow you to move your body in different directions.

Your Muscles

Your bones and joints cannot move by themselves. Your **muscles** (MUS-ulz) help them move. Muscles are attached to your bones. They pull on the bones to make them move.

Muscles help you to lift, push, and pull. Your muscles help with every move you make. The more you exercise your muscles, the stronger they become.

When you kick, the muscles in the back of your leg pull your leg back. Then muscles in the front of your leg pull your leg forward. ▶

YOUR KNEE

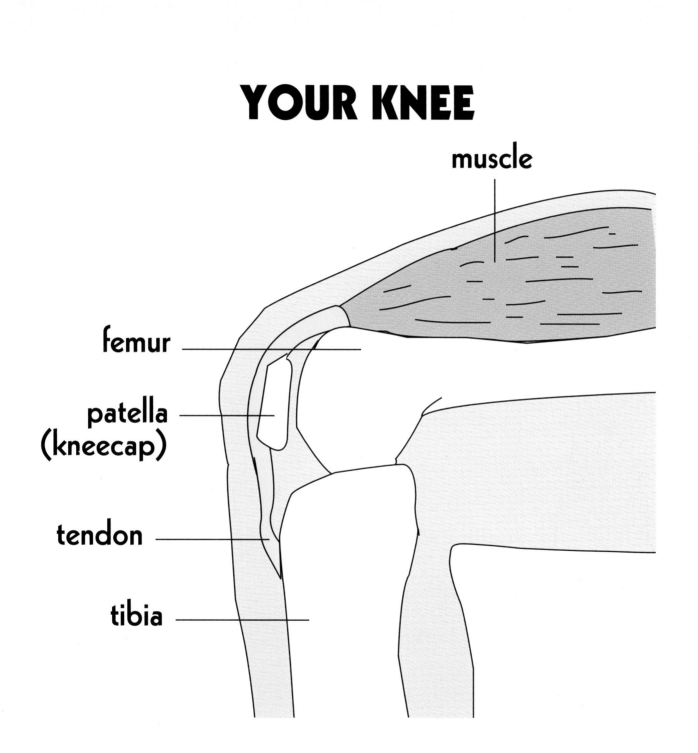

muscle

femur

patella
(kneecap)

tendon

tibia

Your Lungs

Your muscles need fuel to help them move. Where does that fuel come from? Some of it comes from **oxygen** (OX-ih-jin).

Oxygen is in the air. You need oxygen all the time. When you

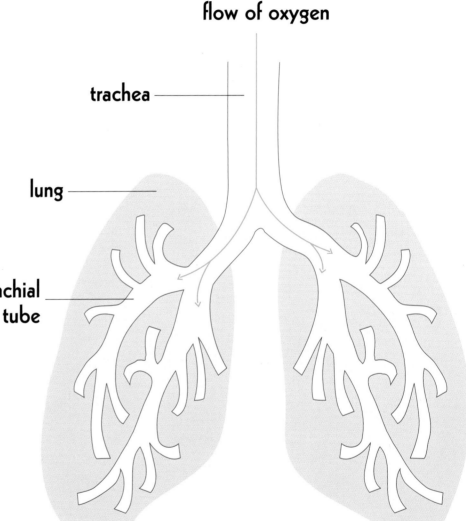

flow of oxygen

trachea

lung

bronchial tube

breathe, your lungs take oxygen into your body.

When you exercise, you need even more oxygen. Your muscles work hard and need lots of fuel. You take deep breaths during exercise to get more oxygen to your muscles.

Exercise makes your lungs healthy and strong.

Your Heart and Blood

Your heart is the most important muscle of all. It pumps blood through your whole body. Blood travels through little tunnels, called **blood vessels** (BLUD VES-ulz).

Blood brings the oxygen from your lungs to your muscles. It brings **nutrients** (NEW-tree-ents) to your muscles too. Your muscles use oxygen and nutrients as fuel to help you move.

When you exercise, your heart pumps harder and faster to bring more fuel to your muscles. Do you ever feel your heart thumping when you run?

YOUR HEART

blood enters heart

anterior vena cava

aorta

blood leaves heart

blood leaves heart

pulmonary artery

pulmonary veins

blood enters heart

heart

posterior vena cava

Each time your heart beats, blood goes into your heart from your body. From your heart, that blood gets pumped into your lungs to pick up oxygen. From the lungs, the blood goes back to your heart. Then, that blood, which is now full of oxygen, gets pumped throughout your body.

Getting Stronger, Going Longer

Muscles get bigger and stronger when you exercise.

Since your heart is a muscle, exercise makes it stronger too.

A strong heart is able to pump more blood to your muscles so that you can exercise, run, or play sports for a longer period of time without getting tired. This is called building **endurance** (en-DUR-ents).

By exercising regularly, you can help make sure that your body is strong and healthy on the inside and the outside.

Exercising and eating foods that are good for you can help you grow big and strong.

Stretch Your Muscles

When you exercise, your muscles do a lot of pulling to help you move. This makes them tight and short. Stretching your muscles makes them long and loose. Loose muscles are flexible. They move more easily and are less likely to get hurt.

Straighten your legs and try to touch your toes. This stretches the muscles in the back of your legs. Stretch gently until you feel a little pull. It feels good!

By standing in this position and pressing your heel toward the ground, you can stretch your calf, or the muscle at the back of your lower leg.

16

It's a good idea to learn how to stretch all of your muscles.

This stretches the muscles in your side and back.

This stretches your hamstrings, or the muscles at the back of your legs. ▶

Exercising Safely

Safety comes first when you exercise.
Remember to:

- ☺ Start exercising slowly. This is called warming up. It helps your body get ready to go.
- ☺ Wear sneakers and loose clothing. It will be easier to move.
- ☺ Stretch. Always stretch your muscles before you warm up and after you cool down.
- ☺ Drink a lot of water. Your body loses water when you exercise because you sweat.

☺ If something hurts, stop. Exercise should not hurt.

☺ Slow down before you stop. This is called cooling down.

To exercise safely, make sure the laces on your sneakers are tied. If you have long hair, pull it away from your face.

Being Physically Fit

Exercising each day and eating healthy foods will help you to be **physically fit** (FIZ-ih-klee FIT). When you are physically fit, your body is healthy and strong and works at its

20

best during exercise and at rest.

Physically fit bodies have:

- ☺ Strong muscles so they can be fast and powerful.
- ☺ Flexible joints and muscles so they can move better.
- ☺ A strong heart and lungs so they can work longer.

Your physically fit body will look good, feel good, and be ready to move!

You may exercise more than you think. If you ride a bike, walk to school, or play games in which you run around, you're exercising!

Choosing Exercise

You can tell the difference between an activity that is exercise and one that isn't. In-line skating is exercise because you're moving around. Riding in a car is not exercise because you're not moving your body.

How can you exercise? You can ride a bike rather than asking for a ride. You can climb stairs instead of going up the elevator.

Exercise is fun. You can ride bikes with your family. Or you can hold a neighborhood Olympics with friends. You can take swimming lessons or join a sports team. Choose exercise for a strong, healthy body!

Glossary

blood vessel (BLUD VES-ul) A tunnel through which your blood flows.

endurance (en-DUR-ents) Being able to exercise for longer periods of time.

exercise (EX-er-syz) Moving your body so your heart, lungs, and muscles work harder than they do at rest.

flexible (FLEX-ih-bul) Being able to stretch and bend your body.

joint (JOYNT) The places where your bones join together.

muscle (MUS-ul) The tissue attached to bones that allows the bones to move.

nutrient (NEW-tree-ent) Anything that a living thing needs for energy, to grow, or to heal.

oxygen (OX-ih-jin) The part of the air that muscles use as fuel to help them move.

physically fit (FIZ-ih-klee FIT) When your body is healthy and strong and works at its best all the time.

Index